Let There Be

9

Enneagram Poetry

Vol. 2

Teshelle Combs

Teshelle Combs Books

Copyright © 2020 by Teshelle Combs

All Rights reserved, including the rights of reproduction in print or online in any whole or partial form.

Manufactured in the United States of America.

Book layout and design by Nate Combs Media.

ISBN-13: 979-8620674916

For the ones who are trying.

Let There Be
9
Enneagram Poetry
Vol. 2
Teshelle Combs

One

Hunter

I do not hope to be good.

I aim for it.

I angle toward it,

Keep it in my crossbow.

I do not try to be good.

I earn it.

Chess

I do not parcel out improvement

It does not come to me in intervals.

It does not come to me at all.

I work, moving all things forward at once.

I move the piece

When the game has already

Been played.

I win the game

Before you knew

We were playing.

Kindness By My Definition

It's not hard for me to

See

The way people could

Grow.

If I could make them

Believe.

They could begin to

Move.

It may not be

Gentle,

But they will be

Better.

Heaven Or Hell

That I see in my mind

All the world and all its ways

And how humans might grow or how they might fail,

But I myself am crooked

Or twisted

Or torn...

I will break the world,

All the while thinking

I have saved it.

What Matters

Principle matters more than drive

Purpose matters more than drills

Progress matters more than pace

People matter more than place.

For I insist they matter.

Two

Empathy

My curse is to others a blessing.

A gift they marvel at

A tool they delight to use.

That I may feel what they feel

Even when I am not looking

Even when they are not speaking

Even when they try to hide it.

I am the one who takes all things

From all people.

Put them inside my heart

And carry them forever.

After which, and whenever you need,

I will carry you.

To Be Needed

I have made a groove

In my heart

From too much pressure

Over time.

That I am needed

And so I must be needed.

If I am not needed,

I will not be needed.

I have made a groove

In my heart

And there is no way

To fill it.

No Matter The End

Love.

Worth the whole ship.

Taking the waves.

Fighting the fury.

Slicing the sails.

When we are going under

And the mast alone remains

And the clouds still have not cleared

And the tempest screams our names,

I will look to where I know the stars

Are hanging still.

And it will have been

Worth it

To love.

Spent

That I will spend

All the breath I have

And the muscle in me

Will be sucked dry

And on the floor

With you near but

Not watching

I will give up

unnoticed.

Magnification

When you are crying,

I will brush the lies away.

When you are broken,

I will keep the pieces safe.

I know without being taught.

I'm certain without being bought.

You are more than you believe

You could ever be.

It is my joy to show you.

Three

See Me

I hope when you

See me you

See much more than I can do

I hope when you

See me you

See much more than I can prove.

I hope when you

See me

You see

What you must

Value.

Rise

It's not that I try

To rise above.

It is more that I must

Rise.

It is worked all through me,

And kneaded into my bones:

Rising,

And also trying.

Do The Dream

The best we can be

Is more than we think.

We can achieve the

Beauty of the arch.

We dream in wings.

We dream in heights.

We dream in dreams.

Worth Unknown

That I should feel sorry.

I should feel guilty.

I should feel something.

But the place my heart lived

Where it used to try to be better

Is now hollow and ashen.

Where there used to be me,

There is now

worthlessness.

Reversed

The world will see

When they look at me

The hopes and dreams

They need to achieve

I am a mirror in motion.

I am the light to be followed.

I am failure reversed

For you.

Four

Mess

Patchwork

Stitched together:

Ambition for thread

And rejection for needle.

I hate my shaky hands

And curse my bleary eyes

As I try to create

An identity

I can call me.

I do this

Unless

I can't.

In dim light

On any given midnight

Alone.

Rejection

Sufficiently great

Worthy of importance

Deserving of note

Any of those would do

Coming to me from you

But all there is between us two

Is condescension,

Inadequacy,

And the open door you walk straight through.

Big And Small

I know what I can be.

Big.

Bigger.

Like a star opening its arms

And hurling galaxies from its chest.

I can be that.

I can.

But I am in my bed

In the tightest ball I can make of me

Unbreathing in my own

Smallness.

I can be that.

I can.

But I am not.

I Love A Good Storm

I'm the one who stepped in

When the warning said

I wouldn't make it out.

At first, it was beautiful.

You cannot know the exact

Color of drowning until you

Give it an honest try.

I did not know that

When I went under

I would not swallow the water

And the water would not swallow me.

Instead, it wiped away

Who I had been

Or who I was trying to become.

I cannot come out of the water now.

For I am no one

Unless I am drowning.

Storms are jealous lovers.

Even If You Never Do

I want you to hold me

Steady.

Let your gaze salvage

Mine.

Tell me you believe my

Name.

Show me you'll be my

Rescue.

Five

Weight Of Independence

Perhaps they think I need another

To link myself to

To carry me through

Like my mechanics don't work

Like my spine is sponge.

But I am carrying

A hundred minds

And I am becoming

Tired of explaining.

Silk

Sometimes I wonder

If the webs I conjure

Will trap me in them.

A spider cannot truly

Endanger itself, I know.

But sometimes I wonder

If sometimes I wonder

Too much.

Scalpel Immobile

Time.

If it's real,

I have always been ahead of it.

Or much too far behind.

I can see without looking

The shapes the world is taking.

I see these things,

The twisting and reforming,

But I do not say them out loud.

So time,

If it's real,

Has always been ahead of me,

Or much too far behind.

Out Of Order

That in one breath

The wind of the unexpected

Will slam through my halls

And sweep up the papers of my mind

Right when I was about to

Do something that

Matters.

Defense

Fists have no utility.

Fury well restrained.

But mind you,

Foolish One.

If you cross me—

I swear—

I will understand

The hell

Out of you.

Six

Present

If you falter.

If you need to lean.

If you feel worn.

Or you are tearing.

You don't need to worry.

I have built your shelter.

I am your shoulder.

I have fetched your water.

I am learning to mend.

You don't need to worry.

My love will do it for you.

Foresight

I don't know if it's

My vantage point

That allows me to see

The danger ahead.

I wish I could not see.

I am glad I can.

Under Constant Companionship

My closest friends

Are quick breaths

And dark clouds.

Either they cling to me

Or I hold to them.

Seems they are

More loyal

Than even

Me.

That I'll need you

And you won't care.

That I'll need you

And you won't be there.

That I'll need you

And will have to go on

Without You.

Warrior

Courage

Never left me

If it's yet to

Find me.

How can it be

There are those

Who wield it

So easily

When my hands

Are only for

wringing.

Seven

More

Hunter

I am.

I don't quite know

Of what.

But I am sure

It will be

More than

This.

There must be

More than

This.

Overextended

When fitting into myself the movement of the tides,

It is important to remain flexible.

Apparently, I forgot to stretch

Before I took on the world.

The Search

If you asked me

What I want in life

I would be too busy

Finding it to

Hear you.

Deprivation

That I am stuck...

And still...

And starving

For something I

Cannot have

With no end

And no point

And no hope...

Perfect Day

Fireworks in my heart

And songs in my head.

A clear day and cloudless

With more than enough gas

And a map I made myself.

Eight

Taking Control

My hands cupped

Around the flame

Are not enough.

I cannot direct something

I cannot take hold of.

So it is I who will form the wax,

Pitch the torch,

And make a way.

Resist

Resistance in itself requires strength.

To resist weakness would mean

Failure is imminent

And I must find the strength

Amidst the weakness

To find the strength.

I will do this.

I will.

On Edge

Pushing is not for breaking.

How can you expect to fly

If I do not get behind,

Both hands on your back

And prove to you

That you can.

My challenge is not

Your demise.

It is your

Destiny.

Predators

That everything I have made,

And all the things I learned,

And every method I enlist,

And all the power I've accrued

Will be taken.

Leaving me

Exposed.

And empty.

And easy prey.

Fire Starter

People treat power like

Hot coals.

Afraid to touch.

Scared to consider.

Power is hot coals.

But I know how to

Hold them right.

I will make fire

From fear.

Nine

Believe Me

Of course,

I believe you.

I have been believing you.

Even if the bones of it all

Fell away,

I would be steady

And I would

Trust you

And believe.

Togetherness

Oh if the outside and the inside of me

The world that shakes and howls

And the mind that rumbles with it

Could find one common truth.

That we could be brought to a place

Where we find

peace.

Preservation

When I have found something good,

Something pure,

Something beautiful,

I will make room

For it to stay that way.

Separation Anxiety

That I will lose my way

Or lose my mind

And need the one who brings me peace

But you will be lost to me.

Inner Peace

Deep down

In the heart of us

Where our souls

Blink open their eyes

And stretch to the sun,

We will find

If we spend the time to look

Our true nature

Bathing in solace

And not in a rush

To leave.

Zero

Prosecution Rests

If I were you,

I would not judge me.

But that's just it, isn't it?

You are not

me.

Architectural Prowess

Don't bother leaving a hammer or nails.

I can make those myself.

After all, you do not know

What it is I'm building.

You go and huddle with

The identities that make you feel safe.

I will be in my shop

Making my own future.

Tests

There is no point to personality.

All the time spent

Measuring and cutting

Instead of moving and living.

You size each other up

But you never become yourself.

Now And Then

There is real work to do

In the gutter places.

In the shadow realms.

In the classrooms.

In the wild.

I will do the real work.

And when I am done,

If you are still counting to nine,

You can tell me how I did.

I will not care

Now.

I will not care

Then

Reborn

You can't keep track of a phoenix, friend.

Right when you think, *ah, here it is about to soar,*

It falls to ash and blows to the earth's ends.

And then, as you say, *oh, what a waste of a bird,*

It is bright enough to bend gravity.

You cannot keep track of a phoenix

Lest it burn you in the tracking

And chill you in the chase.

More Works by Teshelle Combs

Let There Be Nine: **Enneagram Poetry**

(Vol. 1) Poems about the nine possible Enneagram personality types that depict humanity.

For Her

Words laced together on behalf of an idea, a place, a world. Poems for the earth, from someone who's lived here all her life. Poems about what it takes to bring life out of death.

For Him

Words assorted for the robust, for the place we love. Poems about the bold and unafraid nature of nature.

For Them

Poems about the turning of the earth, towards and away from one thing to another, and for the idea of "them," from which we also turn away or towards.

For Us

Poems about the delicate fearlessness of the earth and its beginnings and endings. Perhaps it will give these to us if we are up for the learning.

Love Bad

Poems About Love. Not Love Poems.

A book of poems, by me, Teshelle Combs, for the purpose of the investigation of, or rather the accusation of, or rather the commendation of love and all its claims on me. I would say enjoy, but I am trying to be less naive these days.

Love Bad More

Poems About Love. More Or Less.

A continuation of poems about love by me, Teshelle Combs, in honor of the continuous nature of love and how it goes in either direction, regardless of our requests. I hope this book finds you out of control.

Love Bad Best

Poems About Love. Last, Not Best.

The final installment of poems about love, by me, Teshelle Combs, unless there will be more, which is either up to me or up to love, but probably not up to any of us if poetry has anything to do with anything. You are welcome to it, but I would advise a tentative approach.

Breath Like Glass

Poems for love that never lasts.

Girl Poet

A collection of poems on the passion, privilege, and pain of being (or not quite being) a girl.

Core Series

Ava is the kind of girl who knows what's real and what isn't. Nothing in life is fair. Nothing is given freely. Nothing is painless. Every foster kid can attest to those truths, and Ava lives them every day. But when she meets a family of dragon shifters and is chosen to join them as a rider, her very notion of reality is shaken. She doesn't believe she can let her guard down. She doesn't think she can let them in—especially not the reckless, kind-eyed Cale. To say yes to him means he would be hers—her dragon and her companion—for life. But what if Ava has no life left to give?

The System Series

1 + 1 = Dead. That's the only math that adds up when you're in the System. Everywhere Nick turns, he's surrounded by the inevitability of his own demise at the hands of the people who stole his life from him. That is, until those hands deliver the bleeding, feisty, eye-rolling Nessa Parker. Tasked with keeping his new partner alive, Nick must face all the ways he's died and all the things he's forgotten.

Nessa might as well give up. The moment she gets into that car, the moment she lays her hazel eyes on her new partner, her end begins. It doesn't matter that Nick Masters can slip through time by computing mathematical algorithms in his mind. It doesn't matter how dark and handsome and irresistibly cold he is. Nessa has to defeat her own shadows. Together and alone, Nick and Nessa make sense of their senseless fates and fight for the courage to change it all. Even if it means the System wins and they end up...well...dead.

Contact Teshelle Combs

Instagram @TeshelleCombs

Email: teshellecombs@gmail.com

Acknowledgments

Thank you to those who introduced me to the Enneagram. As a two, it is often difficult for me to know myself. I am often focused on others. Enneagram helped me learn more about my strengths and weaknesses while I studied how to help others. I am learning to be a better person. So thank you to those who studied before me. I hope by writing these poems, I am encouraging others to learn in the same way.